HER INCREDIBLE SURPRISE AND UNSHAKABLE LOVE
FROM JESUS

LEANDRA BISHOP

authorHOUSE®

AuthorHouse™
1663 Liberty Drive
Bloomington, IN 47403
www.authorhouse.com
Phone: 833-262-8899

Published by AuthorHouse 02/23/2021

ISBN: 978-1-6655-1720-1 (sc)
ISBN: 978-1-6655-1724-9 (e)

Library of Congress Control Number: 2021903328

Print information available on the last page.

Modern English Version (MEV) The Holy Bible, Modern English Version. Copyright ©
2014 by Military Bible Association. Published and distributed by Charisma House.

New International Version (NIV) Holy Bible, New International Version®, NIV® Copyright
©1973, 1978, 1984, 2011 by Biblica, Inc.® Used by permission. All rights reserved worldwide.

This book is printed on acid-free paper.

I'M JUST AN ORDINARY GIRL. An average christian. Maybe less than average. I prayed almost every day, and thanked God sometimes. Although as a child growing up, my family raised us to go to church faithfully every Sunday, I no longer went to church. Didn't really think of others, not beyond my family and close friends. Completely just an average working person, who did her own thing. Repeated the same routine every day. Wake up. Go to work. Come home. Work most weekends and some evenings my second job. Typical house work. Time with my spouse. Then repeat. I don't think I realized this at that time, but the repetitious lifestyle had me searching for something I was missing. I don't think I realized it then what that was. Fast forward 3 years later, I'm now divorced and living on my own for the very first time. It was a drastic change in my life. Little did I know then, that my life was not done with the surprising changes.

The loss of my marriage has been incredibly hard. At first, I tried to deny I was in any pain. I simply didn't deal with it at all. I would do whatever possible to keep my mind off of it. For a long time I became obsessed with losing weight. Exercising, eating healthy. Really good for my body, but my mind wasn't coping. Once the divorce happened, I continued different obsessions. Online shopping, reading, dating. Prescribed Xanax I later felt I also had come to rely heavily upon. For me, normal was not in my vocabulary. If I did something, it was often the addictive or the excessive way. Maybe pain increased these already obsessive tendencies. Not coping was the opposite of what I should have been doing. But dealing with my emotions was really hard. Letting myself feel anything was heart breaking. It was much easier to not deal with the loss. To pretend I was back in the past, before things changed. Years ago then, when I was married, if someone would have told me I would end up divorced, I would have told them they were crazy. Of course no one plans to head down a dark, lonely road. Sometimes things happen in life that you don't plan on, and sometimes any insignificances in relationships can be unreasonably magnified during hard times. Without God directing my steps, the marriage broke unnecessarily. Then once I started to let myself feel, because you can't always avoid it, I felt so much sadness and loneliness. My heart felt empty and I felt so alone. The days seemed to drag on and the nights were broken. I didn't feel I had much to live for during that time. I used to be such a person of energy and cheerfulness. I was so full of happiness and light. I then became grumpy, depressed, and just lost. I had no motivation to do much of anything. I spent countless hours at home, reading, playing games on my tablet. I became like a turtle, withdrawn within my own shell. Isolated from family and friends. When I finally began to pray, it began to help, and it was during this time and loneliness that I found myself leaning on God. I started praying more. I started finding myself writing. Normally it was just about anything at all in my life. Anything I was feeling, how my day was, the people I spoke to and how they were helping me through this difficult time. Through my writing, my prayers, and my closeness with God, I began to find the pain becoming more bearable. I started to have hope. It was during these moments that my hope opened up my heart to God to allow Him to start to do great things in my life. To show me something completely unexpected.

During the times after my divorce, the days I would best describe myself as a turtle, at one point withdrew to myself so much that I didn't really talk to anyone. I stayed home and moped. My couch was my best friend. I felt so sad and alone. I felt so pathetic for feeling alone. I felt like I was a loser. I also realized what reason did I have for being so down. Just because a long relationship ended. There were so many people that had it so much worse then I did. In the beginning I was too depressed to see that, but as time went on, I tried to use that as my mantra. During that time of trying to use positivity, I turned to one of my sisters and one of my closest friends for inspiration. Both great women of God, their encouragement and faith helped me to start to slowly build my own. When I would most often talk to one about my worries and my sadness, one thing she would often repeat to me is: "Give it to God!" Easier said than done I thought, but this message became repetitive in my head; especially on the days at home alone, worrying about my future and being on my own, being single, feeling sad. I would so often hear her voice saying this in my mind. It began to help me. It encouraged me to give my burdens to God. This was the biggest struggle I always had and sometimes still have. How often do any of us spend so many days upon days upon days worrying about things we can not control. For me, I struggle with this so much because I don't know how to let God take the wheel. To just remove my burdens and worries to Him. I tend to hold them tight to me like some kind of security blanket. But maybe like anything in life with practice, I could learn to give my worries to Him. I started learning by asking God to show me how to leave my burdens at His feet that He will show me. Honestly I don't think I've ever completely mastered this and I think that's ok. I think God wants me to lean on Him. I think that's what He truly wants of us. He wants everyone to lean on Him. He loves us to focus on Him, because He loves us so much He wants to show this love in the ways He can truly help us and provide for us. How could we ever see God's love or His amazing glory if we never truly lean on Him. So ask Him, and He will help you practice and learn how to lay your anxieties upon Him.

"Do not be anxious about anything, but in every situation, by prayer and petition, with thanksgiving, present your requests to God." Philippians 4:6 NIV

During my sad times, and during those feelings of anxiety and shame, as I struggled to give my anxieties to God and continued writing to help me deal with my sadness, I began thinking of dreams and a calling. I felt so unsure of my future. Of what was ahead for me in my life. I knew one thing I needed to continue to practice. To continue to give my burdens to God. To be still and calm. I knew this calmness helped my feelings, which helped me write what I called at the time: my journal. As I began practicing this, I began to listen for God's voice. I had to practice to distinct the difference of His voice from mine and am still learning this. As I started listening and hearing His voice, one of the first things I ever truly noticed Him telling me on those times when my anxiety was getting to be too much, was to keep my focus on Him. I always worried about everything else going on around me. Having a relationship, being a mom, getting my finances secure. I worried about everything except the best thing I should be worrying about the most. God reminds me to stop worrying about these things and start turning my focus onto Him. I continued thinking of a calling. What was it to me? I thought of my calling helping people. At first I thought it being just at work. Helping patients and students. But then I remembered something I had thought and saw in my mind a while back. The short time I went to church a few years ago, at that time I had been drawing closer to God then also. Then I had a thought and saw myself and one preacher. Him and I were both on a street praying with someone on drugs. At the time when I first saw that in my mind, I thought that I only ever thought that because it just related to a Christian song I had been listening to at the time. Then I wondered if that was supposed to be my calling all along? As I continued to wonder what path I'm headed down and as I have so many questions, I try to find strength and faith in what I'm hearing God telling me: to trust in Him. Even though this is very hard for someone who is completely not used to doing this. But as I hear God tell me and as I continue to practice, I try to stop worrying and over thinking, and just give it to God.

"Jesus looking at them said, With men it is impossible, but with God all things are possible."
Mark 10:27 NIV

As the days went by, there were many days I tried to ignore God. I felt like I could do this on my own. I wanted to be strong and prove to myself I could make it through anything. Those days went by of me ignoring God, when finally I would hear a voice to read my devotional. It was a book my friend had given me. I would also hear the words: "Get your journal." So after ignoring at first, I finally listened. Since I had been ignoring God and isolating myself, I was feeling so lonely again. Making it also harder, was the fact that amongst covid, so many businesses had been closed for a time, and so many of us had to be isolated more. Which I know Satan loved. So after reading the book and writing, and some praying to God, I started feeling better. I felt God wanted to remind me that He made me for a purpose. Sometimes it is hard to follow the path He leads because of sin, sometimes pride; but more often then not, it is Satan. It is an evil voice that tells me I'm all alone now. The enemy's voice that tells me I don't have any friends, or I'm annoying and only annoy everyone. These are lies Satan feeds us and we can not believe them. The enemy knows your weaknesses. He knows my doubts at times I've had about myself and me wanting every one to like me. He only wants to use your doubts against you. He wants to bring out your worse, but remember there is a person you can always rely on to bring out your very best, and that is the Lord. He reminded me that He loves me, that I'm cared for, that I'm important; and all of these things are true for you as well. Most importantly I have learned not to fall for Satan's lies but to always trust God's truths!

...in God I trust, I will not fear; what can a man do to me? Psalm 56:11 MEV

Growing closer to God, I found myself showing more kindness and more calmness. At times, naturally; and other times I had to work at it, because none of us are perfect. I slowly started feeling a weight lifted off my chest. My heart started feeling lighter. I began to laugh a little more. Smile more. I enjoy life more. One of my co-workers gave me a bible that I started reading. With the Corona virus at its worse, it had been suggested to stay home. So I started watching the church services I used to attend, online. One of the first ones I started listening to spoke about trusting in God. It spoke on things I had felt or worried in my heart, but I felt it was just yet another reminder of God telling me that everything was going to be ok. I'm learning that He does that. He will send you suttle, and sometimes not suttle reminders of how He is either working in your life, or there for you through out it. Take time to look for these reminders. If you look close you can see them. Like me, you might miss them. Have it not been for "my journal" I might still have missed them. Noticing them is good because it is His reminder to you that even though things are dark now, and might be for a period, good things are yet to come. Trusting in Him and focusing on Him, love, joy, all of it is yours. He shows that to me as I walk closer with Him. I start to feel His spirit more. I feel His love and it amazes me. It is the same love He has for you, and He won't ever back down from stopping.

> "The Lord has appeared to Him from afar saying: Indeed I have loved you with an everlasting love; therefore with loving kindness I have drawn you." Jeremiah 31:3 MEV

As a couple of months have gone by, my relationship with God had really grown, I began thinking of Him as more of a close friend, and though silly, wondering things like- What is God's favorite food, color? I was thinking How much I loved Him and wanted to Not just know Him as my healer or answer to my prayers, but to know Him deep in His heart. As I was talking to God that I wanted to know Him, to really, really truly know everything about Him, like what He really likes and dislikes; when suddenly I had an image in my mind of Jesus standing in front of me as I sat there. At the time, I was sitting on my love seat in my living room. He was looking down at me. He then put His hand on my right shoulder as He was looking down at me. The image looked a little bit hazy in my mind. I could not see Him clearly. In the image, I could see a man with brown hair, about chin length, basked in a bright white robe. I knew it was Him. In surprise at seeing this, and overcome with emotion, I started crying at this beautiful image. He began to smile as he gazed down at me. I started thanking Him for being there for me. I suddenly had a thought in my mind that He was with me all along. I was thinking that was why I was seeing this, He wanted to remind me of this, and I was beyond moved. Then, the room just changed and became more hazy, with more of a holy, light, and angelic energy. I just felt instead that the image in my head was happening right now. I felt like His hand was touching my right shoulder at that moment. That I could literally feel His hand on my right shoulder. I was totally and utterly stunned. My mouth hung open and I was completely speechless. Tears became pouring down my cheeks. My hand fell over my mouth as the tears flew down. My shoulders and upper body froze out of shock and just feeling in complete awe. He said to me "I have good plans for you." I started sobbing. I started thanking Him and I told Him how much I love Him from every ounce of my body, soul, and heart. I asked for forgiveness for any sins and thanked Him for everything He has done for me including forgiving my sins. I was still sobbing as I told Him I loved Him so much. I heard Him say "Don't cry." So I tried to calm myself and slow my crying, but I was just so emotional. I was unbelievably shocked too. Even after He spoke I continued to sit there motionless, tears continuously flowing down, my mouth hanging open again, and my hand covering my mouth. I was so stunned. I just felt so shocked in disbelief but amazed myself that I was able to speak at all. Then I was asking out loud "Am I crazy?" I was thinking I surely had to be crazy or delusional because surely Jesus Christ would not come down to earth just to visit me. Surely I am losing my mind....were my thoughts. He told me "You aren't crazy." Then what I saw changed and He was suddenly kneeling down and wiping my tears from my right upper cheek. After I felt His hand gaze down my cheek, I began sobbing again, even more stunned then before. I couldn't believe this. I gently touched my cheek beside where I felt his hand. In that moment, I felt such a beautiful and powerful presence of Him. I felt such goodness and warmth. So much love that gleamed off from Him. The shock of this image that I had began to see slightly more clear in my mind, and these literal feelings I was having caused me to tense. My neck and shoulders became frozen again in shock. I was just in awe, maybe a little freaked I guess. He said "Don't be afraid." So I told myself to relax and I tried to relax my shoulders. I was just in total awe and disbelief. I guess I felt so unworthy. So unholy. I have never felt any presence so strong than I did with Him. So beautiful and light. Such a holy presence, and I felt unworthy at the time, which was why I automatically tensed I think, not just out of shock. I guess I felt unholy because of my sins, but looking back now, I don't even know why I felt that way because for not even one second did I feel even a pinch of judgement from Him. All I felt was this powerful light and such sweet kindness that shined from Him, along with this unbelievable endless and overwhelming amount of love that He had for me. It radiated off of Him with such a powerful force. I have never known anyone to look down upon me, an ordinary girl, a sinner, with such kindness and love then Jesus did that day.

Still in total awe and disbelief I was still thinking again, Am I crazy? Then a voice said "You're not crazy" that's when I suddenly saw the image of a tall female angel glowing and bathed in white as He stood beside her. I was floored. Could not believe this was happening. I still felt tense. I felt the angel tell me again "Don't be afraid. Jesus loves you. He is with you. And even though He may not be in the same room with you, He is there. Talk to Him. He can hear you. He will talk to you. He is always there for you." I truly couldn't believe this experience or what the angel said. The words she spoke stunned me! I had been praying about being alone and how sad I felt and how hard it was that even tho I knew that I had Jesus, it was difficult because He wasn't a living man or human beside me that I could physically touch or have contact with, like a hug. It was something I missed since my divorce. After the angel said those words I started sobbing again. I knew they were speaking directly to my heart, and I was beyond touched. Then instantly without even thinking about it, I called out "Come back." What was strange was I didn't even see or feel Jesus leave the room, but it was like my mind instantly knew that He was gone, and I did not want Him to leave. As I still sat there once again, motionless and stunned, my mouth hanging open again, I said again "Am I crazy?" Then I heard the angel say "Trust in Him, Believe in Him." After that, the room was quiet. Peaceful. Then after my shock finally started to lighten a bit, I had the thought that I needed to go write this down.

A little while afterward, still in disbelief, I started to question God. I started to doubt that what I had just experienced had really happened. I know myself well. I over think everything. I tend to doubt myself often. And of course, why wouldn't I doubt this experience. I mean, seriously; like Jesus Christ is going to come to visit this unknown girl?

A hilarious, but crazy sense of humor, sensitive, completely average, not talented at much of anything. Really good at making bad choices. Best talent is being naive and great at making pancakes and microwave scrambled eggs. Just an ordinary girl, an every day sinner. If addictions and obsessing were a talent, I'd win hands down. I'm really just shy, until you get to know me, then I don't shut up. Everything about me is just average. So as I began to question God, He answered me before I could finish asking the first question: He told me "It was real." That I was in the presence of Jesus." He also told me to "Have faith, trust yourself." As I am newly getting closer to God and always question everything, I wondered if that was God I heard, or my own self answering. But I also knew in my heart as I had been getting closer to God, I wanted to help others find the peace that I have been receiving. But as I continued to think on my experience, I knew I could not doubt it. Not what I saw and certainly not what I felt. Not the emotion that came upon me. The powerful energy I felt. The holiness and purity I felt. Also as I thought of the image I was left of in my mind of Him looking down on me, I felt such a beautiful radiance and light that He eliminated. The biggest eliminated thing coming off of Him was love. It just radiated off of Him like waves from an ocean. It was so amazingly strong. There were zero doubts. As I thought about everything I had just experienced, I had no doubt that it was very real.

Then of course in perfect character of me, I then thought how I missed on a golden opportunity. An opportunity to ask Jesus anything I wanted to. Maybe for anything at all. Who knows what I could have discovered or realized. I became so upset with myself. I thought to myself how could you sit there like a moron and not ask Jesus Christ, our Saviour any questions at all. I thought that I blew the one moment in a life time. I was so upset, I started shaking. I really thought I blew it, on finding out something I was supposed to know maybe, or maybe something profound. That is when I heard an angel's voice say "Be still child. That is Satan. Everything happens as its been supposed to." I began to think on that. How Satan is such a manipulator and liar. He wants us to doubt. To question God. To live in fear. To have anxieties. To doubt the existence of Jesus. To not believe any good thing that God shows us to prove that it all is real. Jesus is very real. He lives. He is ours to take. So is His beautiful love and His perfect peace. Take them away from Satan and he will not hold any power over you.

"Peter answered Him and said: Lord, if it is you, bid me come to you on the water. He said, Come. And when Peter got out of the boat he walked on the water to go to Jesus. But when he saw the strong wind he was afraid and beginning to sink, he cried out, Lord, save me! Immediately

Jesus reached out His hand and caught him, and said to him, O you of little faith, why did you doubt?" Matthew 14:28-31 NIV

As a few weeks had past after my experience with Jesus and the angel, and still wondering how in the world did that actually happen, I was beginning to feel stronger emotionally and spiritually. I felt even more love for Jesus. For God. I continued to think on that experience and how incredible and unreal it all was. I cry every time I think about it. I truly did not understand how any of this was happening, but believed God has a plan. Sometimes it's not for us to know everything, but to trust in Him.

So I began repeatedly telling God how much I love Him. I have always had a sense of humor, so I would talk to Him and often joke that He would get tired of hearing that. He began to put this wonderful peace in my heart, which was something I had not felt before, not like this. I never had a feeling of a perfect peace before. A fearless feeling I started to have which came from God, because no one else could ever provide that long lasting peace. I had never been exceptionally close to God; so I had no idea what it truly was or what it felt like. It was a brand new world to me. During these new discoveries, I also found what a positive and wonderful feeling Christian music gave me. Growing up, I never really liked that type of music, but now I have discovered how absolutely wrong I was. There are so many amazing Christian songs and so many songs to match whatever your favorite style is. Not only do they sound good, they are also so relatable to so many people of any age, and in so many of life's many struggles. These songs are inspirational and uplifting. Many are from verses from the Bible. I feel God is using these singers and artists to uplift us and remind us of His love and peace. That's how I felt listening to these songs. So peaceful. On this particular day, I was driving home from work that evening. I was listening to one of my favorite Christian songs at that time: "Where feet may fail" I was simply feeling more and more a deep love and a closeness to Jesus. To God. While listening to the words of the song and thinking about "how I am yours and you are mine" I felt how incredibly true those words were becoming for me. His peace that was presiding in my heart. He was wiping away my anxieties, my fears, my doubts. He proves time and time again that not only can we lean on Him, but He has our very best interests at heart. I was feeling how much Jesus was truly mine. My savior. My provider. My comforter. How I was His. His child to love and to protect. To support and forgive time and time again. As a happiness and peace filled my heart, I became thankful and emotional and started to cry. I began to feel His Spirit so strong it gave me literal goosebumps. I was feeling the Holy Spirit of Jesus. I started thanking Him continuously as tears came down my cheeks. It was such intense feelings. I was amazed by these feelings and I thanked Him again for being with me. He continues to amaze me.

The days following, I felt a peace in my heart more and more. I didn't feel the utter sadness or the depression. During my lonely times, I used to not look forward to the weekends at all. Knowing most people spent them with spouses and kids. But with Jesus, I didn't mind the weekends and I started looking forward to those times to myself. I started to enjoy doing things alone and I didn't think I ever would. Simple things at first, like having a bed and bathroom all to myself. Having my closet to myself, because God knows how many shoes girls love. Slowly after time, it started to become bigger things like going out by myself. With Jesus I started feeling like I wasn't alone. Sometimes I would think to myself, we normally can not see Him physically or His angels, but they walk beside us. They guide us. Through faith, prayer, and the Bible, hope and happiness returned. I didn't feel so lost or afraid of my future. I started feeling emotionally stronger. Everyone is different, but for me, listening to music impacted my life so much. I always loved music, and the more I listened to uplifting Christian songs, the more peace I could feel in my soul. I began feeling the Holy Spirit more and more. My next feeling was a drive home from work. As always, Christian music playing in my car. I often spent time thanking God and praising Him during these times. On this occasion I was listening to music and feeling that spirit. It brings such a beautiful calm and peace in my heart. I continued to thank Jesus for all He has done for me. Even more for His beautiful and strong endless love that I still feel every day when I think about the encounter I had with Him. Songs tend to get me to open up more when I talk to Jesus and I think that might be why they impact me so much. Talk to Him. Listen. Open your heart and receive the peace and endless love He is forever offering.

"For the mountains may be removed and the hills may shake, but My kindness shall not depart from you, nor shall My covenant of peace be removed, says the Lord who has mercy on you." Isaiah 54:10 NIV

As I continue to grow close to God, I find myself as a newbie, learning more and more all the time. I started learning how much He appreciates being thanked when He has done something for us. I stop to think of this a lot. I think about how any of us like to be thanked when we do something for someone. Then to be thanked at how of an amazing job we do for someone is such a rewarding feeling. Imagine how much appreciation God feels when He is validated. Actually really stop and think, even if every small aspect in every day life of what He can be thanked for. Some small things, and some bigger. I think of things like my family, home, work, food, finances. I began thinking of the every day things we might sometimes take for granted, and how some would long for. Eventually I started thinking of even more things to thank Him for. One in particular is the earth and all of the beauty in it. Take a moment and look at your surroundings. Maybe you think there is nothing around your surroundings that's beautiful....Look up. Look at the sky. Look how endless and how you can truly see the amazing work of God. Who else could make such a beautiful blue sky with white puffy clouds and a radiant sun. To wake up to see a morning sunrise, or later see an evening sunset. Even the stars that shower across the sky at night along side with the moon. Think of the rest of the beautiful things we see all around us. The trees, grass, flowers, mountains, the ocean. God showed His love to us in everything around us. I think it is so easy with our busy lives to take for granted these every day. I might be more smitten then most as a lover of nature, but I began stopping for maybe just a few moments everyday to look at the beauty around me and to thank God for His glory. For His love. He could have made the earth an entire dessert, but instead He gave us so much beauty. He shows His love to us in small ways every day. Sometimes we just need to take a few moments to stop and look at those.

"The heavens declare the glory of God; the skies proclaim the work of His hands." Psalm 19:1 NIV

One evening not long after, I was driving home from work listening to music and thanking God for what He has done for me and beginning to bring more happiness back. I continue to try to thank Him often each day. When I was almost home, the image of Jesus with his hand on my right shoulder looking down at me appeared in my head. This memory often will come into my mind, and I absolutely cherish it. It fills my heart with such love and happiness. But this night was different. As I pulled into my driveway, I felt a powerful presence beside of me. Right beside me in my car, and a heat on my right shoulder, warmth. This happened the same time I was having the memory and I felt Jesus was right beside me, in my car. I became emotional. My mouth hung open and a hand over it in surprise. I was not expecting this again. Then like the first time, I could feel myself automatically tense out of awe, shock, and uncleanliness. Relax came into my mind. My words or His, I wasn't sure. I was still learning at distinguishing my voice from His. So I tried to lighten the tension of my shoulders with tears streaming down my cheeks. Completely in disbelief in shock that this was happening a second time, I felt speechless at first. Then once I lightened up my tension, I thanked Jesus for everything He has done for me, for His forgiveness, for visiting me, and for His endless love that has changed my life. I apologized about my mistakes and a thought came into my head that I am on the right path. I continued to cry, more like sob. So swept up in emotion and love and thankfulness for this beautiful person, our savior. As I continued sobbing, I started to say: "You don't know…" Then stopped and chuckled because I thought of course you know, you know everything about me including my thoughts. But I said I'm going to say this anyway: "You don't know how much I love you with all of my heart and all of my soul." During that entire time, I never felt the warmth on that right shoulder leave, and it was just on that shoulder. I didn't feel Jesus leave this time, I just felt such a calm and a happiness. A peace. Still surprised, but I also felt a curiosity to know why I was experiencing these things. I felt such a complete lightness in my car. I thought to myself out loud that I didn't want to get out of my car. So I put my head back on the seat and sat in my car for a while. I wasn't sure why I was experiencing these things, but I felt so unbelievably lucky and thankful to have this experience. As my thankfulness grew, I just felt so, so much love for Jesus. Then for the first time, I actually touched my right shoulder. I never felt it before until then. I don't know if it was because I felt unholy, or just not good enough, but I couldn't bring myself to touch that shoulder fully, not until that night, and when I did, I was totally stunned. Not only did my shoulder feel increasingly warm, but it felt like Jesus put His hand right on top of mine. That I could see this in my mind, Jesus putting his hand on mine and I could faintly feel it as well. I was blown away. I sat in my car, my mouth hanging open once again, stunned. After a few moments, I began again telling Jesus how much I love Him with all of my heart and how I just want to make Him happy. How I want to make Him proud and hopefully draw others to Him and to do good for Him. After a few minutes the image began to fade. Then shortly after, I began to shake off my shock. I then wiped the tears off my cheeks and got out of my car and went inside my home.

Rewind to many years ago, me in my mid twenties. Since those years, I would occasionally sense something dark, a dark presence, and it would be completely at random. Weather or not a person is a Christian, or religious or not, I think we all have that sense in our brains, a little alarm bell in our mind that tells us when a person or a situation just isn't right, or extremely wrong. I think in some cases we can ignore it. But I think there are some of us that can't or don't really know how to ignore this. For me, I didn't know how to ignore this. There are two instances that stick out in my life the very most. On the one instance, when I came into a room I had the sense of multiple dark spirits/demons hovering over a younger man. I not long later came to find out this man was caught on several occasions in public places watching child pornography. The other instance that sticks out to me is me walking to my car, and as I got closer, I suddenly felt that there were several demonic presences, each one outside of every home through out the entire street trying to get into those homes. Then instantly they all stopped, turned their heads and looked right at me. As if they were in surprise that I was looking toward them and they took notice that I noticed them. I had that thought. These times were some of my first instances. At first when these things happened, I thought I was just being dramatic and feeling things that weren't there. My imagination going away from me. Then over the years it continued, but just on occasion. The feelings felt very accurate and those times that they were shown accurate, I later, more recently, began thinking that maybe God gave me a gift to sense these things.

That evening, after my experience again with Jesus, I was home eating dinner. I had already wrote down in my journal about the experience I had again. I was feeling good. I was still in surprise, but I no longer felt bad for not asking Jesus any questions. I simply felt calm and peaceful. I felt good for expressing my deep love for Him. I also felt good for thanking Him for all He has done for me. As I was eating dinner, I felt a dark presence near by. Out of random and at a surprise and a moment when I was feeling so happy and peaceful. Then I heard what I thought was an angel's voice say that "They need more people like me. That I have a gift and a war is coming." I asked a spiritual or a physical war? The voice answered "Both." So then I thought maybe this is why I am experiencing these things. If there is a spiritual war happening, then God definitely wants to help bring people to truly know Him. To experience His goodness and love, and to know they have a forever eternal home. Maybe people that can experience or detect these things, these gifts, can be true eye openers to others.

Afterward, I thought how I never felt that dark presence at all once I heard the angel's voice. I thought of God and how incredible He was and how all of this was playing out. Around that time I was getting a headache, probably from crying so much over my earlier experience that day I had thought. I knew I needed to write this in my journal like all my other experiences. I thought, I really can't yet, my head hurts pretty bad. I laid my head back and with in a minute, my headache was completely gone. I was a bit surprised at this. Then I began thinking of all of the things God had done for me over the last few months. Things that I did not even ask for. Many come to mind. After my divorce, I was concerned about my finances. I didn't know if I could make it on my own. Even working a full time job and a part time job, I had in the past, had some credit card debt, which I had paid down significantly, but it further added to my own debt and regular bills. I thought of a certain approximate amount that I would really like to keep in my bank. Just as a precaution to always have in case I really needed it. Having never even praying for that, six months later, I still have that amount plus a little more. Toward the beginning times of covid, a lot of people around me had received there stimulus checks that were given to us. Everyone around me had received there's. It had been a few months. I knew how much it would help me. Then, the exact day after my ex husband moved into his new home, I received mine. God was providing for me. There were many instances over this time of things He showed He was there for me. That I was not alone. That I could rely on Him. I was starting to learn, like my pastor recently said in our last church service, it's those times when we are at our weakest that we fully lean to God. That is exactly what He wants. He doesn't want a small part or half part, but to lean on him fully. To give your burdens to Him. To forever know that He will always have your back.

"Trust in the Lord forever, for in God the Lord
we have an everlasting rock." Isaiah 26:4 MEV

Later that night, I was thinking a lot about everything that was happening. I never felt the dark presence again once I heard the angel's voice. I began thinking more of myself and what I was experiencing. My greatest personality trait is overthinking. Like typical me, I started to second guess myself. Thinking maybe I was reaching or imagining these things, or trying to cope somehow. So I started questioning if I was right or going too far and asking God to tell me if any of this is wrong. I told Him to please tell me if any of this is wrong. I said that I definitely never wanted to go too far or cope this way, or even more, take the spotlight away from God and use mine and not use His words. I believe God said to me "Pick up your journal." I picked it up. He then said "Show Me anything in this that could possibly be wrong." I began to say maybe the part of me sensing good or evil. He said "Anything that comes from me, you can trust. No bad can come from this. Do not fall for Satan's lies. Trust me." I then thought a God that can move mountains can surely give anyone the gift to sense good or evil more abundantly. I thanked Him and began praying over this journal. Which I have done before, but this time I put it in the air, laid my hands on it, and prayed God's will on His journal. Because this isn't mine. This is His. I just started to realize that this isn't even my journal, it's God's!

As the days continued on, I kept this all to myself, other then sharing it with two of my close Christian friends. I kept thinking people are going to think I'm crazy. Heck, there were times I wondered if I was. I wanted to share these things I was experiencing, but I was scared. I also did not want to put anything into this book that God did not want in it. I continued to turn to music to help with my anxieties and prayer and talking to God and trying to really listen to what He wanted me to do. As I was praying and writing, I asked God again to let me know if I'm doing anything wrong or going off on some imagination. I asked Him to help me remember the important occurances. I felt God answered and said to me There's going to be more occurances. You're going to keep this journal. I began to think of what this was and what it meant. What was God really saying. I began speaking to God again saying This isn't about me or attention. If I can bring one soul to heaven that would be great, but so, so many more would be even better. I worry sometimes I am using this as way of dealing with my pain to cope. God says to me "Go back to your Journal and look at your previous entry." So I did and I didn't have to search far, my eyes immediately fell on the words from God saying "Don't fall for Satan's lies" Out of all the words in my journal, I was surprised that my eyes immediately fell to those words.

I began thinking how I just want to do God's work, not mine. I love Him so much for what He has done for me. For all the endless love He gives in my heart. My body and heart just over flows with this love. It is truly amazing. It is there for you, and for anyone. To know that you are not alone. That He waits for you with welcome arms and an open heart. It does not matter who you are. Your past is gone and a new day can begin with God. He can give you everything you need to deal with life's battles. Strength, hope, courage, and the most endless love and peace you could only imagine of ever having.

I was thinking a lot of these things that happened to me. I asked God in prayer to let me know when He was ready for me to share this story. Meanwhile, sitting on this information was scary at times, thinking about what the future is going to hold, and sometimes I just wanted to shout it to everyone in the streets. I wanted to be like that second person always, but God has to work on me, and still is. Meanwhile life goes on for people, work, family, etc. Things that began seeming odd to me in a different world, a spiritual world that was obviously in turmoil and desperately seeking people to awaken and realize God is here. That Jesus exists and He is here to help you if you just allow Him to. Those work days I found myself in a haze. Like the event over the previous months couldn't really be happening and surely not happening to some ordinary 37 year old girl, who's greatest talent is over thinking and worrying. But God was beginning to change this in me. He still had some work cut out for Him though for sure, but that's ok. So work continues, some days more stressful then others. It's in those moments I find it hard to check myself and use my "be more like Jesus" mantra. One of the following weeks was very stressful. Work, grieving some difficult loss, and not feeling well. Sometimes days will be like this, and I was a little emotional. So that Friday evening I started reading my bible. I wanted to find the chapter I read earlier in the week and found the one I was looking for. Psalm 143 which talks about the enemy "persecuting my soul and making me to dwell into darkness." After reading this I realized this was exactly how I had been feeling. I had been attending Bible study at my church and being with such good people and thoughtful Christians really cleansed my soul as well as the scriptures. Earlier that week, I had begun to open up just a tiny bit. I'm usually very quiet and reserved before I really get to know people. Since then, I felt like Satan was very much trying to attack me because after that day, the week became very hard. Every day seemed like something terrible had happened. When I was thinking about this, I heard "Stop." As I tried to continue reading, but I ignored it at first but then I stopped. I heard a voice say "Close your eyes and focus on Jesus and see Him in your eyes." So I did. I calmed myself. The voice, who at this point I was starting to think an angel, said "Take a breath." I did. "You can do this and be with Jesus any time." That made me teary eyed. Then I began to feel an immense sense of peace. I opened my eyes and talked to Jesus and told Him everything I was thinking and how much I love Him and how thankful I am. How I could never say or show to Him how thankful I am. I felt such a huge peace. I knew without a doubt the Holy Spirit was with me because the most perfect peace I have ever felt in all my life has always came directly from God.

As work became a routine, so did praying, reading my bible, and going to church. I truly believe that God uses chosen people to be our pastors and our priests. That He has annointed ones He has chosen that He knows can speak words of God, faith, His love, the word, and the battles we face in every day life. I felt my pastor was truly one of those all wrapped up in one package. Her services were always refreshing to the soul and reminders of not only ways we can be better for others and ourselves, but also how to face the struggles we have, sometimes each day. A couple of weeks had passed since that stressful week. I still was dealing with some sadness at times. Some loneliness. Was thinking a lot about things in the past that I missed. Later that day as I was reading my bible and praying, I believe God gave me wisdom to know that Satan is trying to get to me and to have me focusing on negative things to keep me from having a close walk with God. There has been countless times when I would begin to pray or read my bible or even go to Church, and I would have negative or bad things happening to me over and over and over again. That is when the enemy likes to mess with us, when he has made us at our weakest. But if we can recognize this as Satan or His minions, we can throw it to God who will gladly deal with them in more then likely an angry way. God does not take this lightly. I also think that sometimes Satan will tempt you with something that you so much desire; and he will make it look so beautiful and shiny with a red bow. Then you either discover two things. One: you are not completely satisfied. Or two: you have been totally and completely tricked. Maybe you have both. Either way, both are temporary. The only permanent and long lasting satisfaction you will ever truly have is from God. That is the only time I have ever felt complete full peace. Nothing temporary. I believe God was reminding me of that this day. When focusing on sadness and pain, that was most definitely Satan bent on keeping me from God and to take away my happiness. One of my good friends always tells me "You've gotta fight for your joy." Sometimes that has been hard and there has been days that I was so tired of crying. So tired of sadness and dealing with pain. But I was reminded that I can't let Satan win. I will fight for my joy! Fight when I am sad. Fight knowing Jesus walks with me and I am stronger then the past and my future is even brighter and stronger with Him.

"Be alert and of sober mind. Your enemy the devil prowls around like a roaring good-looking for someone to devour. Resist him, standing firm in the faith, because you know that the family of believers throughout the world is undergoing the same kind of sufferings." 1 Peter 5:8-9 NIV

Sometimes in those times of trying to fight for my joy, I was learning that maybe sometimes I could ask for some guidance or maybe just some prayers. It's definitely okay to ask for prayers. I was one that definitely didn't like to do this. I didn't like seeming weaker then I already felt I was. But those times that were the hardest, and those times that I asked for prayers, those were the times I could see and feel God moving in my life. Him helping me with my sadness. Him opening doors I did not think possible. Those times made a huge difference. Those time I often could tell people were praying because not only did certain things feel better, but that wonderful peace filled in my heart. I had started feeling depressed greatly again when I started to focus on the negative. Without these prayers, I could feel my old self and deep sadness returning again. I really felt and still do, that deep in my heart, God has a purpose in my life. In the beginning after my divorce, I was going through a lot, so many things that I lost. A lot more then most people knew, and the pain was so harsh. There were times I literally wanted to drive my car off of a bridge. At times in the beginning, I felt the pull to do this very strong. I knew fully in my heart I could not do this, even if the pull at times was strong. Family, friends, and therapy all helped, but nothing ever helped me like Jesus. He brought my joy back and gave my life purpose again. I was so happy I had reached out to have people pray for me. I used to just mask my pain and not really deal with it, or try to deal with it alone, but that couldn't be anymore wrong. I truly hated asking for help or prayers because I also always felt that some dealt with things that were way worse than I that truly needed God's prayers. But God doesn't want us to ignore them. He wants us to confide in Him, talk to Him. Tell Him how you feel and to listen. He will talk to you too. Maybe not every time and maybe not the answers or responses you hope, but God has your back. There is nothing bad that will ever come from God. In me doing this, my closeness with Him has truly began to change me. I truly just want to be a good person, do good for others, and for Him. I want to help let others truly know God and know that YOU ARE NOT ALONE!! You are never alone. God is with you. His son, our savior Jesus Christ walks with you through every battle, every tear, every fear. He is right there. He wants us to believe in this and know without a doubt how precious each person is to Him and incredibly they are loved. I have literally felt the love of Jesus and I can tell you it is overwhelming. I have never felt such amazing love like the love of Jesus. To this day, my right shoulder still radiates His warmth when I touch it. Those days have changed me so much. I want to encourage everyone of this love. I really feel God has chosen me to show others this love to draw them closer to Him, and to know they will never walk alone. During those very emotional times, I thought my world was tumbling down around me. I didn't have Jesus in my center, I barely had Him in my life at all. My world was dark and filled with doubt and negative thoughts. But with Jesus, when I feel doubt or feel emotional, a lot of times I will try to stop, talk to Him, and pray. He is always listening. Every time after, I feel at complete peace.

Later that day I was thinking about my life and my calling, and this book being a part of that. I contemplated if it might be a devotional book. A book that can inspire and encourage others to never give up and to have hope and faith no matter what they may be facing. Then a thought occurred to me that Jesus wants people to come to Him; to notice and recognize Him so much. A vision popped in my head of Jesus standing out in a big city with lots of sidewalks and buildings. There was a huge fountain of water sprinkling out in the middle. Jesus was physically standing right there in the middle, in the center beside the fountain. Countless people were passing by as he stood there and everyone just passed by and ignored Him. Then the thought occurred to me that this is how I felt when I first started having my very bad depression in the beginning. When I felt so alone, like no one was paying attention or noticing me. Jesus doesn't want that. Maybe my understanding of this is another reason I can be brave and do this. I also thought being vulnerable and in an emotional state with such a big and open heart that opens the door to God allowing me these experiences with Jesus. The angels. With Him. I am truly a person that believes anything is possible. I definitely know with God, all things are possible.

"The best is yet to come" God

So, it's October 11th on my finishing writing this. When I first started writing on March 30th, I only did this thinking it was just a journal and a way to help heal and to give my worries to God. WOW--WAS I WRONG! That day on March

30th, 2020 was the beginning of His calling for me....and I HAD NO IDEA! I had never planned this. I never expected or dreamed I could ever experience anything this amazing, but I believe God used me for a purpose. These last several months, I have been feeling this fire inside of me. This blaze deep inside to share this story with everyone. To let people know that Jesus exists! He is the surprise! I could not ask for any better surprise then Jesus!! He is completely without a doubt real. He loves us and will never stop. When you feel like I did, no fight left in your soul, let Jesus fight the battle for you. You will win on earth and eternity.

"My purpose is that they maybe encouraged in heart and united in love, so that they may have the full riches of complete understanding, in order that they know the mystery of God, namely, Christ, in whom are hidden all the treasures of wisdom and knowledge." Colossians 2:2-3 NIV

One thing I will carry with me to the day I die, is that first time that Jesus met me, the last thing I remember is not only the most powerful love He radiated off Him for me, but also how He looked down at me like I was the most precious thing in the world. I have no doubts that this is truly how He feels of each one of us.

.....And to this day, still, when I touch my right shoulder or right cheek on the same spot Jesus did, I feel an amazing amount of warmth and emotion that still comes over me. Like I can still feel it like I did that same day. I just had a realization that I never thought of until right at this moment, me ending this book. But I recall over the last couple of months, me praying to please help me keep this memory. Help me to not forget. Because I knew as time goes on, as years pass by, even memories as precious as this could start to slip away, and I was scared that would happen. I think Jesus answered that prayer and knew that every time I touch my cheek or shoulder, I will remember.

Leandra

ADD ON BONUS:

I was really happy and pretty surprised when I stumbled upon this after this book was finished while I was doing some bible reading.......

"There are various gifts, but the same Spirit. There are differences of administrations, but the same Lord. There are various operations, but it is the same God who operates all of them in all people. But the manifestation of the spirit is given to everyone for the common good. To one is given by the Spirit the word of wisdom, to another the word of knowledge by the same Spirit, to another faith by the same Spirit, to another gifts of healings by the same Spirit, to another the working of miracles, to another prophecy, to another discerning of spirits, to another various kinds of tongues, and to another the interpretation of tongues. But that one and very same Spirit works all these dividing to each one individually as He will." 1 Corinthians 12:4-11 MEV

Printed in the United States
By Bookmasters